COAST
to
COAST

THE BEST OF
TRAVEL DECAL ART

COAST
to
COAST

THE BEST OF
TRAVEL DECAL ART

by ROD DYER & BRAD BENEDICT *text by* DAVID LEES
from the collection of DAVID WILLARDSON

ABBEVILLE PRESS · PUBLISHERS
NEW YORK · LONDON · PARIS

Editor: **WALTON RAWLS**
Designer: **HARRIET BREITBORDE**
Production Supervisor: **HOPE KOTURO**
Library of Congress Cataloging-in-Publication Data

Dyer, Rod, 1935-
    Coast to coast: the best of travel decal art /
Rod Dyer, Brad Benedict, and David Lees.
        p.   cm.
    ISBN 1-55859-156-7
    1. Travel labels--United States--Themes,
    motives. I. Benedict, Brad, 1953- . II. Lees,
    David, 1950- . III. Title.
NC1002.L3D94 1991
741.6'92'0973--dc20   90-22688

DEDICATED
to those anonymous
travel decal artists and
their high-octane souvenirs
of the open road.

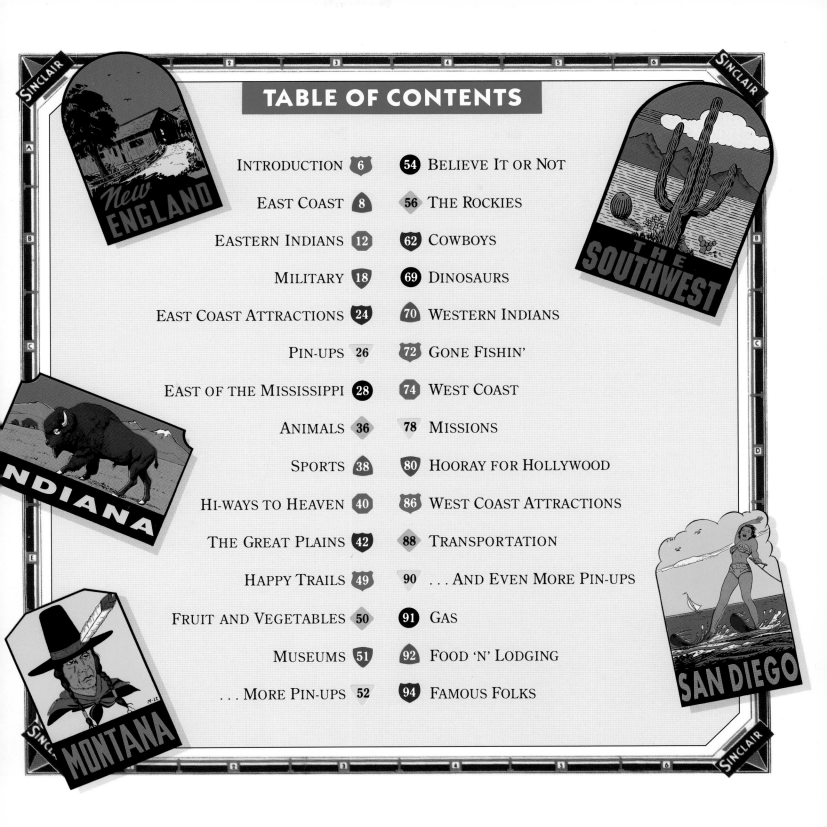

TABLE OF CONTENTS

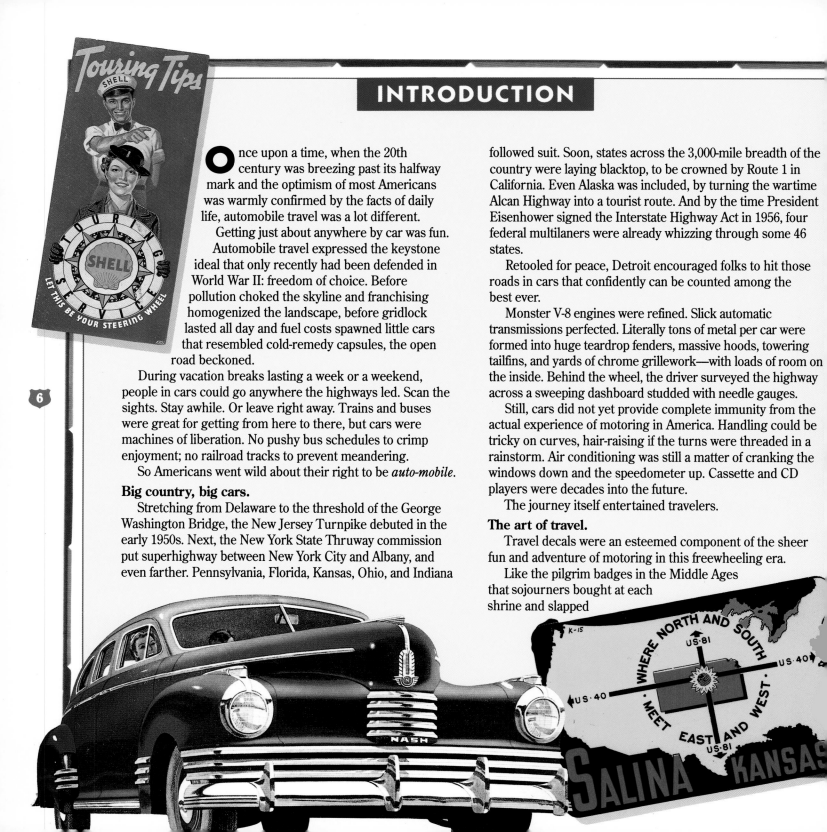

INTRODUCTION

O nce upon a time, when the 20th century was breezing past its halfway mark and the optimism of most Americans was warmly confirmed by the facts of daily life, automobile travel was a lot different.

Getting just about anywhere by car was fun. Automobile travel expressed the keystone ideal that only recently had been defended in World War II: freedom of choice. Before pollution choked the skyline and franchising homogenized the landscape, before gridlock lasted all day and fuel costs spawned little cars that resembled cold-remedy capsules, the open road beckoned.

During vacation breaks lasting a week or a weekend, people in cars could go anywhere the highways led. Scan the sights. Stay awhile. Or leave right away. Trains and buses were great for getting from here to there, but cars were machines of liberation. No pushy bus schedules to crimp enjoyment; no railroad tracks to prevent meandering.

So Americans went wild about their right to be *auto-mobile*.

Big country, big cars.

Stretching from Delaware to the threshold of the George Washington Bridge, the New Jersey Turnpike debuted in the early 1950s. Next, the New York State Thruway commission put superhighway between New York City and Albany, and even farther. Pennsylvania, Florida, Kansas, Ohio, and Indiana

followed suit. Soon, states across the 3,000-mile breadth of the country were laying blacktop, to be crowned by Route 1 in California. Even Alaska was included, by turning the wartime Alcan Highway into a tourist route. And by the time President Eisenhower signed the Interstate Highway Act in 1956, four federal multilaners were already whizzing through some 46 states.

Retooled for peace, Detroit encouraged folks to hit those roads in cars that confidently can be counted among the best ever.

Monster V-8 engines were refined. Slick automatic transmissions perfected. Literally tons of metal per car were formed into huge teardrop fenders, massive hoods, towering tailfins, and yards of chrome grillework—with loads of room on the inside. Behind the wheel, the driver surveyed the highway across a sweeping dashboard studded with needle gauges.

Still, cars did not yet provide complete immunity from the actual experience of motoring in America. Handling could be tricky on curves, hair-raising if the turns were threaded in a rainstorm. Air conditioning was still a matter of cranking the windows down and the speedometer up. Cassette and CD players were decades into the future.

The journey itself entertained travelers.

The art of travel.

Travel decals were an esteemed component of the sheer fun and adventure of motoring in this freewheeling era.

Like the pilgrim badges in the Middle Ages that sojourners bought at each shrine and slapped

NASH

K-15
WHERE NORTH AND SOUTH MEET EAST AND WEST
US·81
US·40
US·40
US·81
SALINA KANSAS

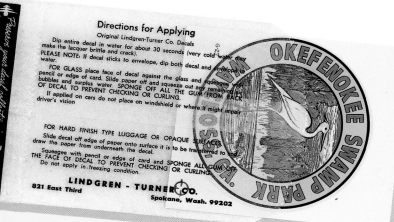

Directions for Applying
Original Lindgren-Turner Co. Decals

Dip entire decal in water for about 30 seconds (very cold water may make the lacquer brittle and crack). PLEASE NOTE: If decal sticks to envelope, dip both decal and envelope in water.

FOR GLASS place face of decal against the glass and squeegee with pencil or edge of card. Slide paper off and squeeze out any remaining air bubbles and surplus water. SPONGE OFF ALL THE GUM FROM BACK OF DECAL TO PREVENT CHECKING OR CURLING. If applied on cars do not place on windshield or where it might impair driver's vision

FOR HARD FINISH TYPE LUGGAGE OR OPAQUE SURFACES Slide decal off edge of paper onto surface it is to be transferred to and draw the paper from underneath the decal.

Squeegee with pencil or edge of card and SPONGE ALL GUM OFF THE FACE OF DECAL TO PREVENT CHECKING OR CURLING. Do not apply in freezing condition.

LINDGREN - TURNER CO.
821 East Third
Spokane, Wash. 99202

onto pages of a treasured Book of Hours, decals proudly declared that the traveler had been somewhere and seen something special. Only 10 cents or a quarter were required to bond roadway memories to the vehicle that had made the trip possible in the first place. Whether meticulously applied to the bumper in an attractively spaced row, or plastered on the rear window with dangerous disregard for visibility, travel decals added to the appeal of auto, truck, or trailer while enhancing the status of the driver.

Few are those who sport just one tattoo, and rare indeed was the auto traveler who displayed a lone decal.

Process and pleasure.

Initially decals were invented for strictly utilitarian purposes, facilitating the decoration of manufactured items that couldn't be conveniently run through a printing press—whether inexpensive dinnerware or locomotives. Decals were also occasionally used to give pine coffins the hefty appearance of marble, or to impart the worldly sheen of lizard to plain leather pumps.

Travel decals, on the other hand, really served no practical end. These minibillboards-on-the-move were designed to be absorbed in a hurry, and production artists at decal manufacturers got the job done beautifully—but anonymously. Their artwork was printed on chemically prepared, porous backing paper and covered with a layer of opaque white ink that was hidden when the decal was transferred to another surface. (Decals to be applied to the inside of windows had their process reversed, with the design

printed over opaque white ink.) Finally the decal was finished with a swash of water-soluble glue. A dip in water would loosen the backing paper and produce a gluey film that would stick the decal to a range of surfaces. Decals can be printed in the standard four-color process but usually are silk-screened to prevent color-fading caused by sunlight.

Travel decal design sensibility is irrepressibly jaunty. Bold illustration, bright colors, flamboyant hand-lettering, and multiple type styles are the hallmarks of travel decals. There's so much happening in each travel decal that the viewer can have no doubt that the place the decal comes from must be terrific. While decals trumpeted all sorts of things—from the virtues of every state in the Union to the security of sundry federal prisons, religion to sex, national monuments to dubious attractions—their true message says embrace America.

Americans were stuck on America. And they stuck these bits of Americana darn near everywhere.

Unfortunately, collecting travel decals has never seemed to catch on in a big way. A few decal printers did sell albums for collectors to display their decals, but no clubs ever got organized, no auctions were scheduled, no experts recognized.

Coast To Coast is the only accessible resource to survey the pictorial delights of these wonderful visuals that help us recall who we were and where we went.

You're invited to stick around for the trip.

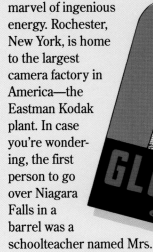

Bunching ganglia of superhighways overlay the Eastern Seaboard and Mid-Atlantic states, giving roadmaps of the region the scary look of an angiogram.

Today, rushing motorists don't have much chance to notice *anything*, except perhaps that while some leaves in New England turn color in the fall, some skins in Florida turn color in the summer.

But during the heyday of auto travel, more time was available to explore. Decal designs depicted the diversity of experience that waited in store, state by state.

Naturally, many decals focused on American history. The *Mayflower* sails again into Plymouth Harbor—her decks curiously devoid of passengers. The crack in the Liberty Bell discloses Betsy Ross's house inside. Lincoln broods over Gettysburg and stares down from his memorial in D.C. Mount Vernon and Monticello rate their own decals. Georgia is home to the Confederate Memorial. Ponce de Leon, searching for the Fountain of Youth, discovers St. Augustine, Florida, oldest city in the United States. The Block House at Fort Kent in Maine is a genuine classic: on this historic site, nothing happened. What's called in Maine "The Aroostock War" was totally bloodless. However, the place is not without import. US 1 starts there, ending in Key West.

It's not all educational, though. Lakes beckon everywhere. New Hampshire has snow. Vermont boasts sugar. New York City is shown as a vertical marvel of ingenious energy. Rochester, New York, is home to the largest camera factory in America—the Eastman Kodak plant. In case you're wondering, the first person to go over Niagara Falls in a barrel was a schoolteacher named Mrs. Annie Tyler. The State House in Providence, Rhode Island, is said to be the second-largest domed structure in the world, runner up to St. Peter's in Rome. Pennsylvania's Pymatunning Lake offers visitors the thrill of buying pieces of stale bread to feed ducks and fish congregating near a spillway. Fish are so numerous, the wily quackers use them as steppingstones to get across the lake.

Danbury, Connecticut. Why the hat? Because the Dodd Hat Shop (founded 1790) immortalizes the history of hat-making. So, what's a "Turtle Crawl"? Hunting turtles accounted for much of Key West's economy until federal protection laws were passed. Captured turtles were kept in pens, or "crawls," before their trip to the cannery. And while in Florida, it is imperative to visit Weeki Wachee; mermaid shows are staged daily. *Oh boy.* Don't forget your swim fins and snorkel!

NEW HAMPSHIRE

The INDIAN HEAD and SHADOW LAKE

NH-20

FRANCONIA NOTCH
NEW HAMPSHIRE

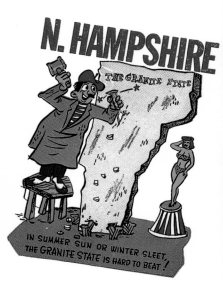

N. HAMPSHIRE

THE GRANITE STATE

IN SUMMER SUN OR WINTER SLEET,
THE GRANITE STATE IS HARD TO BEAT!

BOAR'S HEAD

HAMPTON BEACH N.H.

10

Vt.-17

SUGAR MAPLE

VERMONT

SUGAR HOUSE

BENNINGTON

302 FOOT
BATTLE
MONUMENT!

Vermont

VERMONT

STATE HOUSE

MONTPELIER
VERMONT

VERMONT

MANHATTAN'S
MILKMAN

Mt.
MANSFIELD
VERMONT

CHAMPLAIN'S
DISCOVERY

LAKE CHAMPLAIN

Eastern INDIANS

The Old World shook hands with the New World when the pilgrims landed out east in 1620. It's probably safe to say not much has been the same since, especially for the Eastern Indian tribes. The Mohawk Trail, scene of frightful massacres, is now Route 2, packed during the fall with travelers grimly intent on viewing technicolor foliage. The Wisconsin Dells, hunting range of the Winnebagoes—for real—has turned into a cluster of resorts. A fiberglass statue of Hiawatha, which reportedly stands more than 50 feet tall, beautifies the main drag of Ironwood, Michigan. *Pow. Wow!*

12

IRONWOOD MICHIGAN

COPR LINDGREN TURNER C.

MOHAWK TRAIL
Hail to the sunrise

"You can roam where fancy leads you over hill and dale bu you haven't seen America 'till you've seen th Mohawk Tra

MS-43

MASSACHUSET

WISCONSIN DELLS

DELAWARE WATER GAP
NATIONAL PARK

NEW YORK

AMERICAN INDIAN GRAND COUNCIL
JUNE 21,22,23,1963
WYALUSING ROCKS, PA.
IN THE ENDLESS MOUNTAINS

Z-518

The MOHAWK Trail

INDIAN VILLAGE

CATSKILL NEW YOR

Indian Echo Caverns
CHIEF KUMSEE
HUMMELSTOWN, PA.

15

WEST *Virginia*

V-31

THE FAMOUS HORSESHOE CURVE
NEAR COOL SPRINGS PARK

U.S. ROUTE
50
W. VA.

DELAWARE

DELAWARE

P-14-1

DELAWARE
WATER GAP
NATIONAL PARK

MARYLAND

BIRTHPLACE OF THE STAR SPANGLED BANNER

FORT McHENRY

FRANCIS SCOTT KEY

BALTIMORE *Maryland*

MD-8

MARYLAND

Quite Contrary!

TECUMSEH
FIGUREHEAD
OF THE
USS
DELAWARE

ANNAPOLIS
MARYLAND

MD-6

FORT McHENRY
M A R Y L A N D

17

WASHINGTON MONUMENT
WASHINGTON
DISTRICT of COLUMBIA

Lincoln Statue
Washington D.C.

WASHINGTON, D.C.

MILITARY

Military men rendered in decals seem either spit-and-polish sharp or 100% goofy. Filling the latter category, the guys from Lackland, Leavenworth, Norfolk, and Fort Knox seem to be members of the same family of knuckleheads—peeling potatoes, ogling hula girls, or swabbing the deck. Sea Bees buzz, Marine Corps mutts growl, while first-mates wonder if they'll ever be shipped a-broad—*Sailor beware!*

WEST POINT. N.Y.

LACKLAND AIR FORCE BASE TEXAS

U.S. ARMY

FORT KNOX KENTUCKY

USS BUTTE BE 27

Greetings from CAMP STEWART GEORGIA

U.S. COAST GUARD
CG 40472

Norfolk
VIRGINIA

RAPID CITY
So. Dak.
AIR FORCE BASE

Fort
LEAVENWORTH
Kansas

FT. SAM HOUSTON
Texas

WE ARE A
COAST GUARD FAMILY

PEARL HARBOR
Hawaii
SUBMARINE BASE

US MARINES

FORT BLISS
EL PASO   TEXAS

91 SEA BEES CLUB
CAN   DO
SEABEES
OF AMERICA

U.S. MARINE CORPS
IWO JIMA 1945
SOUTH PACIFIC

U.S. MARINES
PARRIS ISLAND
SOUTH CAROLINA

Welcome!
TO
EPHRATA
WASHINGTON

Sailor
Beware

Virginia

MONTICELLO
CHARLOTTESVILLE, VIRGINIA
V-55

FREDERICKSBURG VIRGINIA

STATE CAPITOL
RICHMOND, VIRGINIA

The Beautiful
CAVERNS OF LURAY
VIRGINIA

THE GOVERNOR'S PALACE

ARLINGTON NATIONAL CEMETERY
ARLINGTON   VIRGINIA

MOUNT VERNON Va.

FAIRY STONE
STATE PARK
VIRGINIA

Williamsburg
VIRGINIA

BIG WALKER LOOKOUT

VA

OLD HUMPBACK BRIDGE

OLD FASHIONED
LOVELY

COVINGTON Virginia

VIRGINIA

20

NORTH CAROLINA

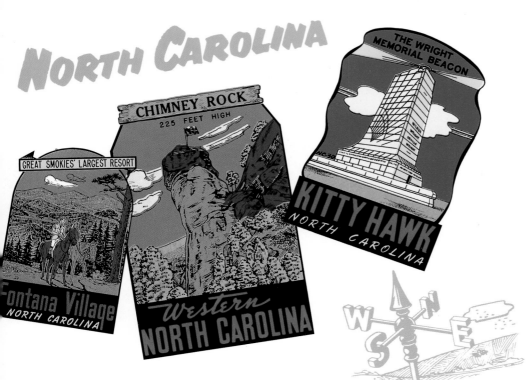

GREAT SMOKIES' LARGEST RESORT

Fontana Village
NORTH CAROLINA

CHIMNEY ROCK
225 FEET HIGH

Western
NORTH CAROLINA

THE WRIGHT MEMORIAL BEACON

KITTY HAWK
NORTH CAROLINA

South CAROLINA

STATE CAPITOL

COLUMBIA
SOUTH CAROLINA

Win a Boy and Save a Man

BROOKLAND
PLANTATION, Inc.
EDISTO ISLAND SOUTH CAROLINA

21

CHAMBER OF COMMERCE INVITES YOU

ARLINGTON
GEORGIA
"THE HUB OF PROGRESS"

EVERYBODY LIKES ARLINGTON

TOCCOA FALLS
GEORGIA

GEORGIA

THE LITTLE WHITE HOUSE
WARM SPRINGS Ga.

CONFEDERATE MEMORIAL

STONE MT. Georgia

PIRATELAND MYRTLE BEACH
SOUTH CAROLINA

COOPER RIVER BRIDGE

CHARLESTON S.C.

East Coast ATTRACTIONS

Obviously, the East Coast has it all. Like the 100-foot electric star brightening the night around the summit of Mill Mountain in Roanoke. The Fountain of Youth on a 20-acre park near US 1 in St. Augustine. The 60-year-old carousel at Glen Echo Park. Nathan's hot dogs on Coney Island. Fantasyland. Dutch Wonderland. Floridaland. Plus the ever-popular town of Intercourse, where visitors can catch a multiscreen audiovisual show about the Amish.

24

HORN'S CARS of YESTERDAY
MUSIC BOX ARCADE
SARASOTA FLORIDA

GlenEchoPark
MARYLAND

THEATER OF THE SEA
ON THE FLORIDA KEYS

LOOK OUT FOR SPLASH

Plain & Fancy Farm

FLORIDA

FLORIDALAND

Fountain of Youth ST. AUGUSTINE FLORIDA

LAND

PLAIN & FANCY FARM and DINING ROOM
INTERCOURSE, PENNSYLVANIA

Dutch Wonderland

Dutch Wonderland
LANCASTER, PA

ER, PENNSYLVAN

Beautiful FANTASYLAND
GETTYSBURG
PENNSYLVANIA

CHILDREN'S ZOO &
ELECTRIC STAR
MILL MOUNTAIN, ROANOKE, VA.

25

CONEY ISLAND
NEW YORK

Pin-ups

Honeys of the highway constitute a road hazard—an attractive nuisance—whether they are as sweet as maple syrup in Vermont, classy chassis built in Michigan, babes in the woods in Maine, or Kentucky babes. Every darn one is a decal doozy, most definitely see-worthy—and there's more to come. *Hubba, Hubba!*

27

This is the benchmark region.

They've got the Big River, the Mississippi, flowing nearly 4,000 miles from the headwaters of the Missouri to the Gulf of Mexico. They've got the Big Seam, in Alabama, largest deposit of iron ore in the southeast. They've got the Big Horse Race, the Kentucky Derby. They've got the Big Car Race, the Indianapolis 500. They've got the Great Lakes, the Grand Ol' Opry. The World's Biggest Cheese is in Ohio; the World's Biggest Six-Pack in Wisconsin. Three of the world's tallest buildings have Chicago addresses.

In addition to the muchness glaring from either side of the highway, travel decals showcase alternate wonders. On US 31, the Vulcan Statue stands grisly watch over Alabama's traffic. After any fatal car accident, the green light glowing in Vulcan's hand burns red for a full day. Henry Ford's first Model T was built in Detroit, Michigan, in 1909. Across the lake in Wisconsin, guests who partied at the Villa Louis (circa 1870) were weighed before

and after they dined. The host and hostess wanted to be sure everybody got enough to eat and drink. Decal fanciers admire natural and constructed bridges, sniff tulips, watch paddleboats chug on by, put hayfever on hold.

If you think about it a minute, modesty is only common sense. In this neck of the nation, the road leads not only to Devil's Lake . . . but to Hell its own self.

KY-6

KENTUCKY
THE BLUEGRASS STATE

DOWN SOUTH

A TOWN ON ITS WAY UP

ALL THE WAY TO HELL AND BACK

HELL MICH.

Alabama

BELLINGRATH Gardens
near MOBILE · ALABAMA

NATURAL BRIDGE of ALABAMA

BIRMINGHAM Ala.
VULCAN
GOD of FIRE and METAL

Beauvoir, near Biloxi, Mississippi,
last home of Jefferson Davis.

29

VICKSBURG Mississippi

ME FORGET?
HELL NO

DIXIELAND

STATE CAPITOL JACKSON
MISSISSIPPI

OLD COURTHOUSE MUSEUM
VICKSBURG
MISSISSIPPI

BILOXI
MISSISSIPPI
MIS-B

Mississippi

Tennessee

DAVY CROCKETT BIRTHPLACE
TE-64
LIMESTONE, TENNESSEE

"Down in Dixie"
LUMBER
COTTON
INDUSTRY
MEMPHIS
Tennessee

"GENERAL"
CHATTANOOGA
Tennessee
CHICKAMAUGA DAM

RANDALL
Greetings from
GREAT SMOKY MOUNTAINS
TE-29

See 7 STATES from Point Lookout
UMBRELLA ROCK
LOOKOUT MT. · CHATTANOOGA · TENN.
ALABAMA KENTUCKY VIRGINIA NO. CAROLINA SO. CAROLINA
GEORGIA TENNESSEE TENNESSEE

SHILOH National MILITARY PARK

FORT DONELSON TENN

GRAND OLE OPRY
NASHVILLE, TENN.

STATE CAPITOL

FRANKFORT, Kentucky

U.S. GOLD DEPOSITORY

FORT KNOX
KENTUCKY

Kentucky

My Old Kentucky Home BARDSTOWN
KY.

31

CUMBERLAND FALLS

KENTUCKY

KY-36

CHURCHILL DOWNS

FROZEN NIAGARA

KY-8

MAMMOTH CAVE
National Park
KENTUCKY

LOUISVILLE Kentucky

OHIO

COLUMBUS · Ohio

THE DAYTON SPEEDWAY STOCK CAR RACES

HIGH BANKED
DUST FREE
PAVED TRACK

4

FRI. NITE.

1550 SOLDIERS HOME ROAD – DAYTON 18, OHIO

OHIO

the Buckeye State

ZANESVILLE Ohio

"THE FAMOUS Y BRIDGE"

OH-9

32

Q♥

TERRE HAUTE
INDIANA

QUEEN CITY OF THE WABASH VALLEY

IN-4

Q♥

INDIANA

BROWN COUNTY

NASHVILLE INDIANA

INDIANAPOLIS 500 SPEEDWAY

CHICAGO ILLINOIS
WRIGLEY BUILDINGS

ILLINOIS

Lincoln's Home...
SPRINGFIELD, Illinois

The HEART of ILLINOIS

CHICAGO
ILLINOIS

Peoria
ILLINOIS

MICHIGAN AVE
Chicago
IL-4

CHAIN o' LAKES
ILLINOIS

STARVED ROCK
STATE-PARK
ILLINOIS

CHICAGO
ILLINOIS

33

STAND ROCK

WISCONSIN

THE BADGER STATE

WISCONSIN

SCENIC NORTHERN WHITE WATER STRETCH OF FAMOUS WOLF RIVER
TROUTLAND
EXCELLENT CANOEING & TROUT FISHING

WISCONSIN
Dells, WIS.

WISCONSIN DELLS
WISCONSIN

HISTORYLAND
OLD CLARK HOUSE
CLARK HOUSE
OLD HAYWARD
HAYWARD WISCONSIN

35

DEVIL'S LAKE
WISCONSIN

12 TROUT STREAMS
ALL WELL STOCKED
Lakes
IRON RIVER WISCONSIN
IRON RIVER
In the Heart of Vacation Land
A PARADISE FOR
HAY FEVER SUFFERERS

STATE CAPITOL at MADISON
WISCONSIN

VILLA LOUIS
PRAIRIE DU CHIEN, WISCONSIN

WISCONSIN DELLS, WIS.
SIGHTSEEING BOATS

ANIMALS

Can anybody really tell us why the bald eagle is our national animal? Nobody anyone knows has ever seen one, unless the bird was featured in a nature documentary or mounted behind glass. Consequently, we have pledged our allegiance to other critters. American travel decals are a vast trophy room of the rare and exotic beast, tracked down during highway safaris. Delicate deer, amorous mules, hypertrophic rabbits, alligators, butterflies, snakes, and the jackalope are only some of our prized fauna. We don't want to hunt them; we desire only to flatten their decal likeness on vehicle or valise. Which is a heck of a lot better than flattening their cute little selves on the roadway.

I'M FOR
NGUS

Desert of Maine
ME-17

Yellowstone Cub

GLACIER
National Park

FOLLOW THE MONARCHS TO
BUTTERFLY TOWN, U.S.A.

PACIFIC GROVE
MONTEREY PENINSULA - CALIF.

HOME OF THE
QUINTS

S-3-3

ABERDEEN
SOUTH DAKOTA

REPTILE GARDENS
RAPID CITY
SOUTH DAKOTA

WILD STALLION

Palo Duro Canyon

TEXAS

WISCONSIN
AMERICA'S DAIRYLAND

1000 ANIMALS

NEW   YORK
LAKE PLACID

What!
'e're in...   Us worry?

ARABOO
ISCONSIN

DESERT SWEETHEARTS

C-63

CALIFORNIA

ROADRUNNER
PARK
T-113

ALPINE, TEXAS

NM-79

JACKALOPE

NEW MEXICO

SPORTS

Sports are never out of season in America. And decals work up a sweat showing that sports are never dull either. Amateur player or pro squad mascot all seem to be winningly grinning. Travel decals with athletic accents prompt the recollection that the hi-way has long been the main channel delivering sports, bringing skiers to the slopes, or the visiting team to town. Maybe that's why, even in this era of flight, an out-of-town game played by local heroes continues to be called a road trip.

SWIM

EVANS PLUNGE
HOT SPRING, SO. DAK.

PUGET SOUND

Washington

C-241

CALIFORNIA

Balboa Island
CALIFORNIA

SEASIDE HEIGHTS, N.J.

FLAMINGO
SKI SCHOOL
& SURF SHOP

Z-1029

WHITE WATER CANOE RACE
WORLD'S END STATE PARK — ENDLESS MTS., PA.

TAOS
SKI VALLEY
N. M.

BELLEAYRE MT.
SKI CENTER
PINE HILL, N.Y.

WINTERHAVEN
FLORIDA

GREEN BAY

WI-76

GREEN BAY

MILWAUKEE

41

WISCONSIN

THE MIAMI
DOLPHINS

M

CHAMPIONS
1956   1957

FOLLOW THE
FLYERS

The Rose Bowl

PASADENA CALIF.

"DEM BUMS"
Brooklyn

DODGERS

CINCINNATI
REDS

MILWAUKEE

Home of the

BRAVES

Cleveland

39

New York

YANKS

BROOKLYN

CONEY   ISLAND

Dodgers

BROOKLYN
BRIDGE

NEW YORK

Pittsburgh
Pirates

Chicago

CUBS

INDIANS

HI-WAYS to Heaven

Faith propels the motor-borne adventurer as much as gasoline does. Relying on a machine with thousands of critical moving parts, facing blinding distances on uncertain turnpikes, trusting the competence and sanity of other drivers—and actually looking forward to the trip—calls for steadfast belief. Auto travelers do not meekly hope they'll get where they're going, they know they will. *If that isn't faith . . .*

ST. CHRISTOPHER BE MY GUIDE

Santa's Chapel NORTH POLE NEW YORK

Church of the TRANSFIGURATION JACKSON HOLE, WYOMING

LDS

PASSION PLAY

LAKE WALES FLORIDA

SAINT ODILIA
Shrine of St. Odilia ONAMIA · MINNESOTA

EISENHOWER PLACE of MEDITATION
ABILENE, KANSAS

Shrine of
Our Lady of the Mts.
BRETTON WOODS · N.H.

Shrine of the Madonna
QUEEN OF THE UNIVERSE
EAST BOSTON, MASS.

THE
LITTLE BROWN CHURCH
NASHUA, IOWA

SANCTUARY OF OUR SORROWFUL MOTHER
THE GROTTO PORTLAND OREGON

ST. ANDREWS
EPISCOPALIAN
CHURCH

ATLANTIC CITY
WYOMING

ZEPHYR
POINT
PRESBYTERIAN
CONFERENCE
GROUNDS

PREACHING
CHRIST CRUCIFIED,
RISEN AND COMING AGAIN

FIRST
BAPTIST
CHURCH
CLEARFIELD, PA.

GLORIETA · BAPTIST · ASSEMBLY
GLORIETA
NEW MEXICO

St. Pierre Et St. Paul
LEWISTON · MAINE

41

THE GREAT PLAINS

Traveling by car, bus, or train through the Central Standard Time Zone can be a disorienting experience.

Hills, those friendly geological markers measuring distance gone and distance to go, take a sabbatical. Except for parts of the Dakotas and Texas, the landscape motif is 2-D. Flat. Mercilessly flat. Flat enough that tales are told of homesteaders suffering violent seasickness while transiting miles and miles of nothing but prairie grass waving across their retinas. The scarcity of obstacles requiring a detour means that roads could be used as rulers. Miles tick by at their own pace, unimpressed by horsepower. The horizon is what there is to see.

Nevertheless, it would be a mistake to figure the region for not much more than a whole-grain wilderness.

The population center of the United States is in Missouri; the geographic center of our land mass is in Kansas, the Sunflower State. Mount Rushmore's 60-foot high faces and the Crazy Horse Memorial are in South Dakota. A sculptor who collaborated on

Mount Rushmore then undertook the chiseling of a 500-foot likeness of Crazy Horse and his pony out of a granite mountain in 1940.

In Tulsa, the musical *Oklahoma* is performed six days a week, every week of the year. In the Ozarks, "Land o'the Mountain Dew," the Great Arkansas Outhouse Race happens each October. The Municipal Rose Garden in Tyler, Texas, perfumes the air with its nearly 40,000 bushes.

The travel decals cooked up in and around America's breadbasket are leavened by these slightly out of kilter goings-on. Decal artists persist in skirting the edges of decorum, and, sometimes, good taste. A good trick in the domain where the center is the preferred location.

Ford '50' V-8

DES MOINES *Iowa* STATE CAPITOL

WATERLOO IOWA

HOME OF THE NATIONAL DAIRY CATTLE CONGRESS

IOWA

LAKE OKOBOJI IOWA GREAT LAKES *funland* U.S.A. IOWA

KANSAS

DODGE CITY KANSAS

"MY TRAILS HAVE BECOME YOUR HIGHWAYS"

SEVEN MILLION HEAD OF LONGHORNS MARKETED from 70's to 80's

EST. 1859 OLD SANTA FE TRAIL

FORT LARNED NATIONAL LANDMARK

KANSAS

NEBRASKA

BUFFALO BILL'S HOME TOWN

FORT CODY NORTH PLATTE, NEBRASKA

HOME ON THE RANGE

AUTHOR'S CABIN

KANSAS STATE SONG

45

MISSOURI

STATE CAPITOL

JEFFERSON CITY MISSOURI

Bluebird STATE BIRD MISSOURI

The SUNFLOWER STATE

KANSAS

GENERAL STORE 1869

Old Abilene KANSAS

SALOON

K-21

RAZORBACK
ARKANSAS

X-2p
LAND O' THE
MOUNTAIN DEW

ARKANSAS

FORT SMITH, Ark.

America's own
AR-11 SPA
HOT SPRINGS
National Park
ARKANSAS

AR-3
EUREKA SPRINGS
ARKANSAS
IN THE OZARKS

TURNER TURNPIKE Entrance
TURNER TURNPIKE
TULSA-OKLAHOMA CITY, Okla

OKLAHOMA
OK-10
WILL ROGERS
1879 — 1935
Claremore

OKLAHOMA
OK-20

SEQUOYAH
STATE PARK
ON LAKE WAGONER
WAGONER
OKLAHOMA

COAST TO COAST
TRAILWAYS

NATIONAL
COWBOY HALL OF FAME
OKLAHOMA CITY, OKLAHOMA

OIL CAPITOL
TULSA
OKLAHOMA

47

GREETINGS FROM "So Big TEXAS

© J.R. Willis

G-17 DD

Texas LONG HORN
WIDTH OF HORNS 9 FT. 6 INCHES
THE BLACKEST LAND
GREENVILLE THE WHITEST PEOPLE

MADE IN TEXAS BY TEXANS

"ROSE GARDEN OF AMERICA"
Tyler TEXAS

Gateway to Old Mexico
BROWNSVILLE TEXAS

Treasure Island GALVESTON TEXAS
T-65

THE OLD LIGHTHOUSE
PORT ISABEL TEXAS

WELCOME TO
THIS IS GOD'S COUNTRY DON'T DRIVE THRU IT LIKE HELL
HONDO TEXAS

THE ALAMO TEXAS
SanAntonio

PADRE ISLAND TEXAS

HAPPY TRAILS

There are roads and there are roads, but some superhighways are superstars. The Santa Fe Trail went from New Mexico to Independence, Missouri, as the prime Old West trade route between the United States and Mexico. It's so famous, a 40s western film bears its name. The Pony Express also spawned a movie and a television series. Folklore describes the Donner Party munching on corpses during their trip to California. However, the all-time cement celebrity is Route 66, with a hit song—"Get your kicks on Route 66"—and a smasheroo 60s TV series. Known now as I-65, its former name still lingers.

Old National Trail

U.S. 40

COPR. HUGH V. McKEE

"WITH MY BANJO ON M'KNEE"

The DONNER Trail ON U.S. HIGHWAY 40 CALIFORNIA

66

I GET MY KICKS OUT OF ROUTE 66

ROUTE 66

Santa Fe Trail

49

Navajo Trail

PONY EXPRESS Trail

"MADONNA OF THE TRAIL"

ROUTE 40

APPALACHIAN TRAIL

"THE OLD OREGON TRAIL"

FRUIT
& VEGETABLES

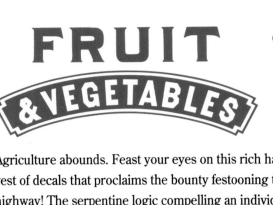

Agriculture abounds. Feast your eyes on this rich harvest of decals that proclaims the bounty festooning the highway! The serpentine logic compelling an individual who is also a licensed motorist to purchase a decal of a humongous spud for the car is unclear—but need not detain travelers from making plans to see King Cotton crowned in Memphis in early June or scheduling a drive along the Golden Spike Fruitway in Utah for Peach Day on the weekend after Labor Day. Apples and oranges. Tomatoes and potatoes. Cherries, cranberries, carrots, and pears. And *Yes, we have no bananas.*

MUSEUMS

None of these here is exactly the Louvre, but travel decals produced on their behalf promise a much more interesting time. Who could pass up the graphite reactor at Oak Ridge? Designated a National Historic Monument in 1966, it is the only government-owned reactor the public currently has a chance to see up close and personal. The Circus Museum in Baraboo puts on live big top shows; rival Ringling Museum in Sarasota is a sprawling complex of theaters and art museums camped on the grounds of the estate of the late John Ringling. Ripley's is probably worthwhile as well. Like the decal says, it's air-conditioned. After all, peering at oddities for a couple of hours straight is hot work.

PORTSMOUTH NAVAL SHIPYARD MUSEUM

PORTSMOUTH, VIRGINIA

PIONEER AUTO MUSEUM
MURDO, SO. DAK.

Ripley's Believe It or Not! MUSEUM
AIR CONDITIONED
ST. AUGUSTINE
FLORIDA

RINGLING MUSEUM
SARASOTA · FLA.

CIRCUS WORLD MUSEUM
BARABOO, WISCONSIN

ATOMS WORKING FOR YOU
AGRICULTURE
MEDICINE
INDUSTRY
AMERICAN MUSEUM of ATOMIC ENERGY
OAK RIDGE, TENNESSEE

GETTYSBURG NATIONAL MUSEUM
HOME OF THE ELECTRIC MAP
GETTYSBURG, PA.

THUNDERBIRD MUSEUM
HATFIELD, WISCONSIN

ARIZONA SONORA DESERT MUSEUM
ARIZONA

CIRCUS WORLD MUSEUM
BARABOO, WISCONSIN

...more Pin-ups

PIKES PEAK or Bust

NEW MEXICO

LOUISIANA

Some Bundle

IOWA

OKLAHOMA

NEBRASKA

THE NEW OIL STATE

NORTH DAKOTA

A MUTOS

PRINTE

SOUTH
DAKOTA

HUNTER'S
PARADISE

KANSAS

ARIZONA

COLORADO

53

HIT THE DECK

LADY LUCK

LADY LUCK

A♠
A♠

NEVADA

ARKANSAS

Stepping High in
IDAHO

BELIEVE IT OR NOT!

Trust us. The Big Stack in Anaconda, Montana, is the largest freestanding brick structure on earth; the Washington Monument could easily slide right up inside the thing. Lakeview, the tallest spot in Oregon, sits 4,800 feet above Lake Albert, dwarfing Wisconsin's highest peak, 1,950-foot Rib Mountain. St. Augustine was established in 1565, oldest city built by Europeans; the oldest wooden schoolhouse dates from the 1800s. The Homestake Mine in Lead (where William Randolph Hearst's daddy first got rich) is one of the biggest gold mines in the Western Hemisphere. As for Odessa's declaration that it contains the largest farmers in the world, their daughters and sons of the soil don't seem any bigger than other farmers anyplace else.

54

M-32

WORLD'S LARGEST COPPER SMOKE STACK AND PRODUCING SMELTER

CONTAINS 9,300,000 BRICKS

SPORTSMAN'S PAR

ANACOND

MOST BEAUTIFUL FERRY CROSSING IN AMERICA

M.V. VALCOUR

VALCOUR

STREAMLINE FERRIES

LAKE CHAMPLAIN

OLDEST HOUSE IN U.S.A.

SANTA FE
NEW MEXICO

WORLDS HEAVIEST LIFT BRIDGE

HOUGHTON-HANCOCK. MICHIGAN

RIB MT. STATE PARK
WISCONSIN'S HIGHEST PEAK

76

THE HOMESTAKE
WORLD'S LARGEST GOLD MINE
LEAD
SO. DAKOTA

THE WORLD'S ONLY
CORN PALACE
MITCHELL
SO. DAKOTA

OLDEST STARS AND STRIPES FLAG IN EXISTENCE
BENNINGTON MUSEUM · BENNINGTON, VT.

MD-10   WORLD'S THIRD LARGEST
ESAPEAKE BAY BRIDGE · Md.

32 FT.
LARGEST HAND-DUG WELL
109 FEET
WATER   25 FT.
THE BIG WELL
GREENSBURG, KANSAS

THE TALLEST TOWN in OREGON
LAKEVIEW WELCOMES YOU

HOOVER DAM

WORLDS LARGEST PETRIFIED WOOD PARK
HIGHEST IN THE WORLD (727 feet)
LEMMON SOUTH DAKOTA

55

nt.

LARGEST FARMERS IN THE WORLD
COULEE DAM
SPOKANE
ODESSA
Heart of the Big Bend
WE LIKE ODESSA   SO WILL YOU!
ODESSA
WASHINGTON

OLDEST WOODEN SCHOOLHOUSE IN U.S.A.
ST. AUGUSTINE, FLORIDA

DRAKE WELL PARK & MUSEUM
P-86
WORLD'S FIRST OIL WELL DRILLED 1859
TITUSVILLE, PA.

Sail the LOST SEA
WORLD'S LARGEST UNDERGROUND LAKE
NEAR U.S. 411 - U.S. 11
in EAST TENNESSEE

"Thar's gold in them thar hills"—sometimes. Oftentimes fortunes were made in mining valuable resources other than *precious* metals. For 50 years, copper gave Butte, Montana, the right to call itself "the richest hill on earth."

In Tombstone, Arizona, "the town too tough to die," early silver miners were warned they'd find their tombstones quicker than they would silver. One smart-alecky prospector then dubbed his first rich claim "Tombstone" to gall the doubters.

It used to be that the Rocky Mountains were the ultimate chastity belt protecting virgin territory from land-horny settlers. Getting over them has never been an easy trick. Peaks hit the clouds at average elevations that are, well, Rocky Mountain high. A single state in the range, Colorado, charts more than half a hundred

summits cresting over 14,000 feet.

Many aspects of going to such lofty heights haven't altered, at least so you could tell, from one automotive era to the next. It's at least theoretically possible to motor for a full day out in the boonies without seeing another driver. Cars need sturdy radiators to ward off a dreaded boil over in the thin atmosphere, and checking your brakes while on the flatlands is also prudent.

Breathtaking vistas fill any window not obscured by decals. The wide-open spaces of the mountains are both wide and open; within them, road explorers will discover Mesa Verde, the Sawtooths (or is it teeth?), Yellowstone, and the Grand Tetons. Westering farther will disclose the Grand Canyon, Santa Fe, Taos. Not to mention Vegas!

The atmosphere may be thin, the scenery may induce oxygen deprivation, but the attitude most everywhere is down to earth. If you don't believe it, chance a gander at the decal from Kellogg, Idaho.

48270

56

LINCOLN'S SILVER $ BAR & GIFT SHOP HAUGAN, MONT.

E PLURIBUS UNUM 1921

MONTANA

MONT A-A-A-NA

HOME OF URANIUM MINES

BOULDER MONTANA

GLACIER National Park MONTANA

The RICHEST HILL ON EARTH! BUTTE, MONTANA

THE OLD STAGECOACH WELLS FARGO & CO.

VIRGINIA CITY · Montana

IDAHO "GEM" STATE

Sun Valley IDAHO

You are now near KELLOGG The Town which was Discovered by a JACKASS — and which is inhabited by it's Descendants.

KELLOGG, Idaho

GHOST TOWN

BLISS IDAHO

Frontier Ghost Town

SUN VALLEY Idaho

COLORADO

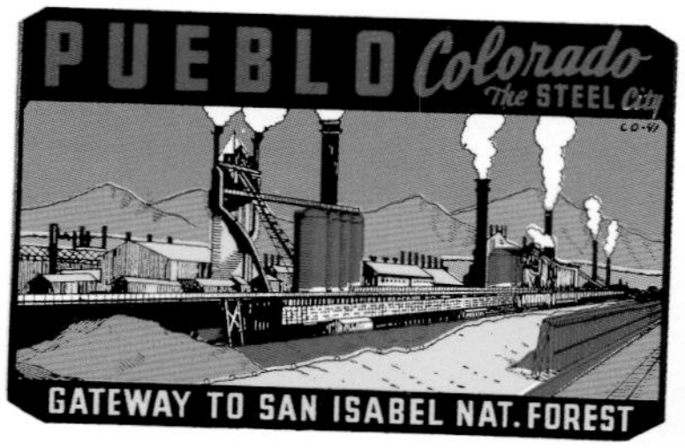

PUEBLO *Colorado*
The STEEL City
GATEWAY TO SAN ISABEL NAT. FOREST

ELEVATION 9280 ft.
HOME OF THE HARD ROCKERS HOLIDAY
SILVERTON
COLORADO

THE FACE ON THE BAR ROOM FLOOR
CENTRAL CITY
Altitude 8500 ft. COLORADO

COLORADO

COLORADO

TOPS THEM ALL
ALTITUDE 14,110 ft.
PIKES PEAK REGION
Colorado

PIKES PEAK OR BUST

GARDEN OF THE GODS
COLORADO SPRINGS, COLORADO.

WYOMING

YELLOWSTONE PARK "OLD FAITHFUL"

NORTHEAST ENTRANCE
YELLOWSTONE *Park*

Yellowstone
NAT. PARK

Shy Anne FROM
ANNUAL WORLD FAMOUS "FRONTIER DAYS"
CHEYENNE WYOMING

WYOMING
HOME ON THE RANGE!

BUFFALO *Wyoming*

DEVIL'S TOWER WYOMING

BIG HORN COUNTRY WYOMING

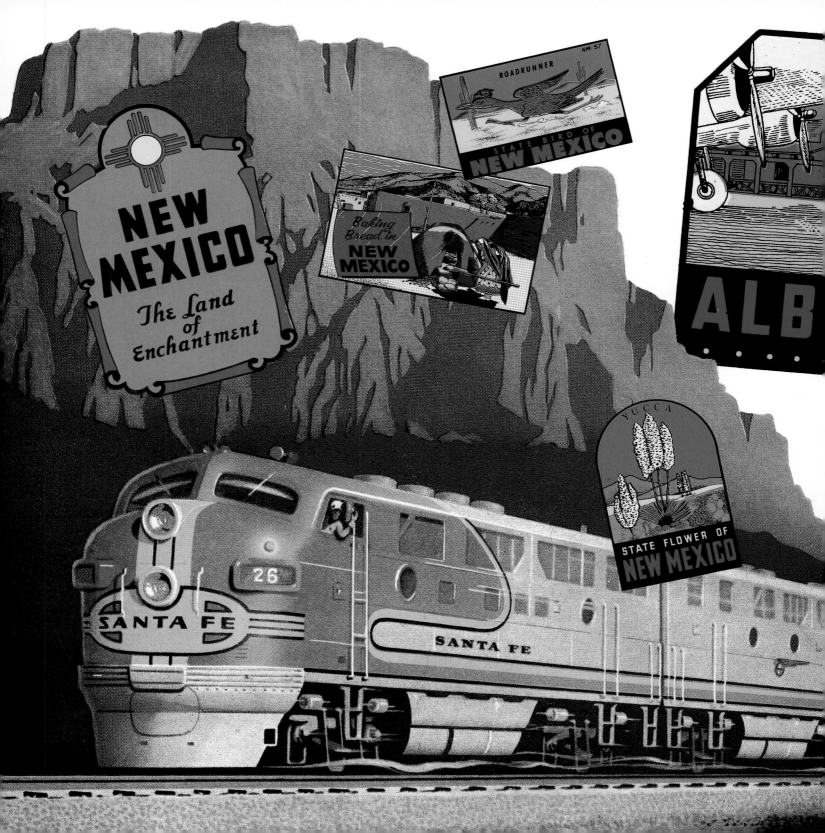

BOWLIN'S
RUNNING
INDIAN
NEW MEXICO

BLUEWATER
DEMING
CONTINENTAL DIVIDE
RUIDOSO
GAGE
AKELA
ALAMOGORDO
FAIRACRES
LAS CRUCES

Z-344

AZTEC RUINS *National Monument*
N E W   M E X I C O

GALLUP
NEW MEXICO

GALLUP, N.M.
INDIAN CAPITAL
INTER-TRIBAL
INDIAN
CEREMONIAL
AUG 11-14

UERQUE
New Mexico

THE STATE CAPITOL

SANTA FE   N E W
MEXICO

Albuquerque NEW MEXICO
U.S. 66

NM-10

PUEBLO DE TAOS
N E W   M E X I C O

NM-6

NM-29

WHITE SANDS
MISSILE RANGE
NEW MEXICO

CARLSBAD

CAVERNS
New Mexico...

GOVERNMENT SPRING

TRUTH or CONSEQUENCES ·N.M.

CIMARRON, N. MEX.

COWBOYS

At the end of The War Between the States, out-of-work veterans were drawn by the lure of earning $30 a month convincing stinky, stubborn cattle to plod along trails stretching from deep in the heart of Texas to railroad towns hundreds of miles away.

By 1895, the cowboy era was over. But the cowboy legend was ready to ride. Rodeos awarded points and purses to cowboys who could best translate their skills into athletic performance. Dude ranches lent a refined whiff of the corral. Rootin' tootin' decals rounded up the whole shebang, leaning heavily on the motif of men, horses, and flying hats. *Saddle up, pard. Let 'er buck!*

LET 'ER BUCK

PENDLETON OREGON
The Round-Up City

TOMBSTONE ARIZONA

MEMBER
Oregon
CATTLEMEN'S ASS'N

HITCHING POST
for the DUDE RANCHES
Victorville·Calif.

RODEO
CLOVIS·Calif.
LAST WEEK-END IN APRIL

Historic DEADWOOD S.D.

TEXAS

B BAR T RODEO
WISCONSIN DELLS
WISCONSIN

WILD WEST TOWN
MAPLECREST, N.Y.

OLD FORT SPOKANE
WASHINGTON

UTAH

SALINAS
RODEO
JULY 18 TO 21 ST.

OMAK
WASHINGTON

ARIZONA
INTEREST AND TOURING MAP

TOMBSTONE
ARIZONA
THE TOWN TOO TOUGH TO DIE
BILLY CLANTON
TOM MCLOWERY
FRANK MCLOWERY
MURDERED
on the Street
of TOMBSTONE
1881
BOOTHILL GRAVEYARD

WATCHTOWER
A-16
GRAND CANYON
National PARK
A R I Z O N A

LAND OF CACTUS ....
OCOTILLO
SAHUARO
PRICKLY PEAR
CHOLLA
BARREL CACTUS
RAINBOW
SPANISH YUCCA
MESCAL
PHOENIX, ARIZONA
NM-41

"ON THE TRAIL"
GRAND CANYON
National Park ARIZ.
A-21

Marriage License
In know all men by this Certificate
Yuma
Arizona
A-11

WONDERLAND
OF ROCKS
A R I Z O N A

PAINTED DESERT
ARIZONA
A-61

65

A-3
Home of
ARIZONA SNO-BOWL
SAN FRANCISCO PEAKS
FLAGSTAFF
ARIZONA

Nevada

GATEWAY TO PYRAMID LAKE
SPARKS, NEV.

BOULDER DAM

EL CAPITAN
GAMBLING HALL

HAWTHORNE
NEVADA

LAS VEGAS
NEVADA

RENO, NEVADA

RENO
THE BIGGEST LITTLE CITY IN THE WORLD

MESQUITE
Nevada

66

68

Greetings from UTAH

WHERE THE SUMMER SUN SPENDS THE WINTER
ST. GEORGE
UTAH
DIXIE SUN BOWL

UTAH
POINTS OF INTEREST
AND TOURING MAP

ROADSIDE GEYSER
UTAH

BONNEVILLE SALT FLATS
NEAR GREAT SALT LAKE

BIG ROCK CANDY MOUNTAIN
On U.S. Highway 89—6 miles north of MARYSVALE, UTAH

DELICATE ARCH
ARCHES
National Monument
U T A H

GOLDEN SPIKE NAT'L HISTORIC SITE
PROMONTORY SUMMIT Utah

AT YOUR SERVICE FROM CANAD
STANDARD
RON G

TEMPLE SQUARE
SALT LAKE CITY Utah

DINOSAURS

Thunderbeast Park. Lost World. Prehistoric Gardens. Enchanted Forest. Their names are as wondrous as the dinosaurs they exhibit. Some parks show replicas, some the real McCoy, some are themselves extinct. They are the Dino-lands. Presenting a peek at times unimaginably ancient, permitting motorists to say thanks to the animals whose remains are the source of our gas and oil.

Western
INDIANS

Vagabonding by car through the West, travelers fancy themselves intrepid pioneers moving 'cross Injun Country in their motorized prairie schooners. Decals were sold to offspring of immigrants who dropped in for a peek at the only original Americans. Out West, Indian heritage can be experienced through travel decals displaying colorful folklore and traditions. Stepping to war dance rhythms, crafting pottery, noodling on drums, and making papooses. Cruising home with a carload of Southwest souvenirs, were these tourists enlightened by their trip?—*And How!*

71

Gone Fishin'

We can't seem to forget we came from water eons back. Water is essential to human life, *critical to affixing decals*. We may not be able to become part of the sea ever again, but we sure can make the sea part of us. Florida sailfish. Minnesota walleye. California whales. Dolphins in South Dakota. That giant razorback clam swallowing Oregon Shores. Hooked, speared, harvested, or gazed at, it's fair game for travelers and travel decals. Besides, decals attest to the veracity of the fish stories told when home port is reached, and the water becomes a memory once more.

WESTPORT, WASH.
WE FISH WITH...
TRAVIS CHARTERS
Phone 268-414

FLORIDA DEEP SEA FISHING

HOME OF THE BLACK HILLS PASSION PLAY
SPEARFISH
SOUTH DAKOTA

ADIRONDACK mts.
NEW YORK

VACATION PARADISE
INDIAN HEAD COUNTRY
WEBB LAKE
WISCONSIN

PORTLAND ZOO
OREGON

CACHUMA LAKE

Lake KABETOGAMA WALLEYS
IN NORTHERN MINNESOTA

LIMIT YOUR KILL
IEFFC
DON'T KILL YOUR LIMIT!
INLAND EMPIRE FLY FISHING CLUB

Pelican
KLAMATH FALLS

JUMBO CRAB

DEPOE BAY
OREGON

OCEAN AQUARIUM
GIANT OCTOPUS
HERMOSA BEACH
CALIFORNIA

Silver Sands Motel
POINT PLEASANT BEACH, N.J.

Watch the Seals Perform
SEASIDE AQUARIUM
OREGON
o-55

OREGON SHORES

SEA WONDERS Alive
CRESCENT CITY, CALIFORNIA.

MARINE LIFE
5-66
RAPID CITY
IN THE BLACK HILLS
OF SOUTH DAKOTA

The left coast is where the highway ended and the dreams began.

Automobile travelers, decals tell us, could find Hope on the border with British Columbia, Peace in Washington—and visit the arch built to honor it. They could fish Canada's Peace River, and ponder the audacious vision of Oregon loggers who could send a six-centuries-old tree crashing to the forest floor in a mere six hours.

On the Western boundary of the country, decals cataloged a whole bunch of dreams that revolved around the sun. A decal from Alaska advertises the Midnight Sun, but neglects to note the unremitting darkness shadowing the rest of the seasonal clock. Dune scooters cavort in their convertible down the banks of the Oregon Coast Highway. Curvaceous Mexican beauties shine beneath blazing skies.

Understandably enough, helioculture hits its apex in California. Palm Springs, Catalina, a nameless beach with a lecherous Old Sol leering at a sand sprite—the sun reigns. Almost the only Californians not able to snag sun rays were the inmates of Alcatraz prison.

Hawaiian decals show off the sundrenched charms of the tropical territory. The only drawback being that nobody has yet figured out how to pave the Pacific.

But no matter. The highways out West are dreams in themselves, say the decals. One marvelous decal touts Los Angeles's "Spectacular Freeways" as an attraction worth seeing.

SOUTHERN CALIFORNIA
ALL-YEAR CLUB VISITORS BUREAU · 505 W. 6th ST. · LOS ANGELES

GAS
LAST CHANCE

SIGNAL GASOLINE

AT DEALER OWNED STATIONS...
from CANADA to MEXICO

74

WASHINGTON

SEATTLE·Wash.

EIRAM
L.O.S. OF NA
SPOKANE, WASH.

space needle

SEATTLE, WASH.

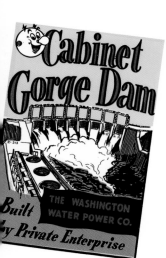

Cabinet Gorge Dam

THE WASHINGTON WATER POWER CO.

Built by Private Enterprise

MT. RAINIER

GINKGO
PETRIFIED FOREST
VANTAGE
WASHINGTON

PUYALLUP
HOME OF WESTERN WASH. STATE FAIR

INTERNATIONAL PEACE ARCH
BELLINGHAM
WASHINGTON

SEATTLE WORLD'S FAIR
1962

ATOMIC ENERGY PLANT

The HANFORD WORKS
RICHLAND PASCO KENNEWICK
WASHINGTON

SEATTLE, WASHINGTON
MONORAIL

GRAND COULEE

OREGON

ASTOR COLUMN
ASTORIA
OREGON

Woodland Deer Park
CAVE JUNCTION, OREGON

CAPE FOULWEATHER
O-100
OREGON COAST

WE'RE WILD ABOUT OREGON
Especially...
GRANTS PASS!

REDWOOD Empire

The Dune Scooters
Oregon Coast Hwy.

600 YEARS OLD AND 6 HRS. TO FALL

EUGENE Oregon

UNDERSEA GARDENS
NEWPORT, OREGON

OREGON
STANDARD OIL
ROAD MAP

AUTHORIZED DISTRIBUTOR
STANDARD STATIONS INC

Travel with us
AMERICA'S FAVORITE

Missions

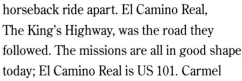

Introducing their chain centuries before Howard Johnson had the idea for his, Franciscan padres Junipero Serra and Fermin Lasuen knit together Spanish California by building 22 religious settlements paced about one day's horseback ride apart. El Camino Real, The King's Highway, was the road they followed. The missions are all in good shape today; El Camino Real is US 101. Carmel

Mission cradles the tomb of Father Serra. Yes, the swallows do return to Capistrano on or about March 19. Mission building in Arizona gets more mixed reviews. Tumacacori Mission was never completed, plagued by bad winters and feisty Apaches. Missionaries were impolitely asked to leave Mission San Xavier del Bac in the late 1820s, coming back around the turn of the century to preach to the Indians—a practice that is still followed.

N JUAN CAPISTRANO

1776

Mission San Luis Rey
CALIFORNIA

C-145

Mission San Miguel

SAN MIGUEL, CALIFORNIA

C-43

San Carlos Borromeo Mission
CARMEL, CALIFORNIA

TUMACACORI Mission
ARIZONA

San XAVIER DEL BAC Mission
ARIZONA

OLD MISSION
SAN JUAN CAPISTRANO
C-176

EL CAMINO REAL

79

Hooray For HOLLYWOOD

"Where you're terrific if you're even good." Hollywood was a farm town when it was settled in 1903, joining the City of Los Angeles in 1910. Three years later, Cecil B. DeMille lensed *The Squaw Man*, the first feature film ever made in Hollywood. During the apex of auto touring, Tinsel Town was still the capital city of dreams. Stars were in the sky, on the sidewalk, strolling the streets. Hollywood decals packed their own special magic—transferring that star status instantly. Lights, camera, action. *Roll 'em!*

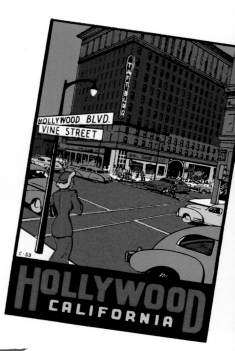

NIAGARA FALLS

VANCOUVER
Trappers

HOPE
BRITISH COLUMBIA

SAULT STE. MARIE
U. S.
CANADA

PEACE RIVER
ALBERTA

Greetings
FROM
CANADA

The Great
NORTHWEST

CANADA

RANCHEROS VISITADORES

MEXICO

ENSENADA
MEXICO

OLD MEXICO

"the fun spot
South of
the Border"

Cactus PETE'S
JACKPOT NEVADA
ON HIGHWAY 93

JUAREZ
MEXICO

MEXICO

BUENA PESCA-Good Fishing*
ENSENADA B.C.
OLD MEXICO

Home of the Fabulous 5-10
MADE IN U.S.A.
CALIENTE
TIJUANA, MEXICO

85

WEST COAST ATTRACTIONS

Mickey & Minnie. Bubbles the Whale. The Birdman of Alcatraz. Frankenstein and his bride. From Disneyland to Marineland. From cellblock tours to movie studio tours—and you thought the East Coast had it all!

Alcatraz was the retirement home of entrepreneurs Al Capone, Machine Gun Kelly, and Robert Stroud, "The Birdman." Ex-maximum security slammer, "The Rock" is now a tourist attraction in San Francisco Bay. You can experience the flavor of the Wild West at Ghost Town in Knott's Berry Farm. Pan for gold, witness an old-time train robbery, and chow down on fried chicken and Mrs. Knott's boysenberry pie . . . *Mmmmm!*

FAMOUS ONE-"LOG" HOUSE

UNDERGROUND GARDENS FRESNO, CAL.

THE PLACE FOR FUN
Pacific Ocean Park
SANTA MONICA, CALIF.

UNIVERSAL CITY STUDIOS

-"LOG" HOUSE
WOOD HIWAY · CALIF.

Bubbles

MARINELAND OF THE PACIFIC

CALICO GHOST TOWN
1881
YERMO, CALIF.

PAUL BUNYAN'S BLUE OX "BABE"
TREES of MYSTERY
REDWOOD HIWAY, CAL.

PAUL BUNYAN
TREES OF MYSTERY
SHRINE OF THE REDWOOD HIGHWAY

7734
ALCATRAZ

7734
ALCATRAZ

87

TRANSPORTATION

Of course, driving from one fabulous sight to the next can't claim exclusivity on the total roving experience. Frustrated by speed limits and state troopers, motorists could fly above it all on airplanes. Hop aboard amphibious contraptions in Arkansas. Ride the dog. Take the Freedom Train or the locomotive to Oblivion. Watch rockets' red glare. Travel aboard either a frigate or nuclear sub. (Although that remains a fantasy trip best left to the imagination of decal artists.) Then, back on the road again, hoping not to get stuck behind any Redwood Hi-way logging truck, nor in front of any member of the American Racing Drivers Club. *Brrrrm!*

LOS ANGELES INTERNATIONAL AIRPORT

R.M.S. QUEEN MARY
PORT OF LONG BEACH
CALIFORNIA

...IT'S FUN TO FLY!
ATLANTIC FLIGHT SERVICE INC.
CHARLOTTE, N.C.

See HOT SPRINGS, ARK. by LAND and WATER
FUN AND ADVENTURE ON THE WHITE DUCKS
GAY-D
LAND AND LAKE TOURS

88

MOBILE
Alabama

U.S.S. NAUTILUS
·FIRST ATOMIC SUBMARINE·
NEW LONDON, CONN.

AMERICAN RACING DRIVERS CLUB

MACKINAW CITY
MICHIGAN

WESTWOOD RACING CIRCUIT
BRITISH COLUMBIA

BONNEVILLE Salt FLATS
UTAH

MACKINAC ISLAND

Z 529

Greyhound POST HOUSE

WORLD FAMOUS 1880 TRAINS
HILL CITY - OBLIVION - KEYSTONE   SO. DAKOTA
S-50

FIRST SHIP OF   THE U.S. NAVY

U.S. FRIGATE CONSTELLATION
BALTIMORE, MARYLAND 1797

Cable Car

C-31

SAN FRANCISCO
CALIFORNIA

Original LOG HOUSE
REDWOOD HIWAY · CALIF.

89

96

4412

Daylight

4412

OMPOC
ALIFORNIA

C-219

SPIRIT OF 1776

FREEDOM
IS OUR JOB!

FREEDOM TRAIN

ARCADE & ATTICA
Steam Railroad

ARCADE, N.Y.

... and even more *Pin-ups*

OREGON
O-43

AVALON
SANTA CATALINA

Santa MONICA
CALIFORNIA

SAN DIEGO

WAIKIKI
HAWAII

ALOHA
Hawaii

WASHINGTON

STAGE COACH INN

SOUTHERN FRIED CHICKEN

22968 Sierra Hwy., Newhall, Calif.

Phone NEwhall 259-0282

CALIFORNIA

BAJA
CALIFORNIA

90

GAS

Hitherto, topping off the gas tank and cleaning the windshield was a bigger deal than outpatient surgery is now. Attendants came scurrying in their spiffy white uniforms emblazoned with thick embroidered logo patches. Gasoline was, apparently, actually sexy in San Diego. Why, even the two stiffs selling gas in Lovelock got dressed up to practice their profession.

Check the oil and fill 'er up.

FOOD 'N' LODGING

Now and then on the auto-route, unsuspecting voyagers found themselves saddled with two unwelcome hitchhikers named hunger and fatigue. Coffee shops and motels were there to care. Families who felt bushed didn't need to be concerned with the frazzled state of their appearance to receive respite from the road. Dinner clothes were not required for dinner; advance booking was never needed for a room. Motels featured air-conditioning, swimming pools, magical beds that delivered bumpy massages. At many roadside restaurants the car could be gassed while the family grubbed. Food. Shelter. Fuel. *Simply . . . drive in.*

TOP HAT / DRIVE IN E. 2101 SPRAGUE

Pea Soup ANDERSEN'S RESTAURANT BUELLTON CALIFORNIA

THIRD AND SUNSET BLVD. SPOKANE RI. 7-5713 Panda SELF SERVICE DRIVE-IN

LUMBERJACK CAFE FLAGSTAFF, ARIZ.

CLIFTON'S LOS ANGEL California

Wilson's MINT CANYON restaurant CALIFORNIA

Menu

BIG BOY

GRAND HOTEL MACKINAC ISLAND, MICH.

FREEMAN'S CAFE EVANSTON HOTEL EVANSTON, WYOMING

LITTLE AMERICA
HOTEL · LODGE · CABINS · BAR · COFFEE SHOP · FOUNTAIN · GAS & OIL
Wyoming's Newest Travel Center on U.S. Hiway 30, Wyoming

Timberline Lodge
in MT. HOOD NATIONAL FOREST --- TIMBERLINE, OREGON.

SMOKYLAND MOTEL
Glenn Glass

MANY GLACIER HOTEL
GLACIER NATIONAL PARK, MONT.

REDWOOD MOTEL
RT.1, Box 137C WISCONSIN DELLS, WISCONSIN
Z-675

"IN THE BEAUTIFUL CATSKILL MOUNTAINS"
The HOTEL WALTERS
CAIRO · NEW YORK

E VISITED HOWARD JOHNSON'S "HOST OF THE HIGHWAYS"
OHIO TURNPIKE U.S.A.

ROUGH RIDERS HOTEL
MEDORA, N. DAKOTA

FISH LAKE LODGE
FISH LAKE, UTAH

93

Chieftain
HOTEL MOTEL
NEAR THE BOAT DOCKS·
WISCONSIN DELLS, WIS.

BIG SUR Lodge
BIG SUR, CALIF.

Famous Folks

Hails from a mountaintop in Tennessee, killed hisself a bear when he was only three. Shot by Jack McCall during a poker game in Deadwood. His grave is the same height as his name. Penned "My Old Kentucky Home" while visiting someone else's. Major loser. Major winner. Born at Sinking Spring Farm. Buried in Lexington. Famous folks, surely; they are: Davy Crockett, Wild Bill Hickok, Mark Twain, Stephen Foster, General George Armstrong Custer, Chief Sitting Bull, Abe Lincoln, and Man O'War.

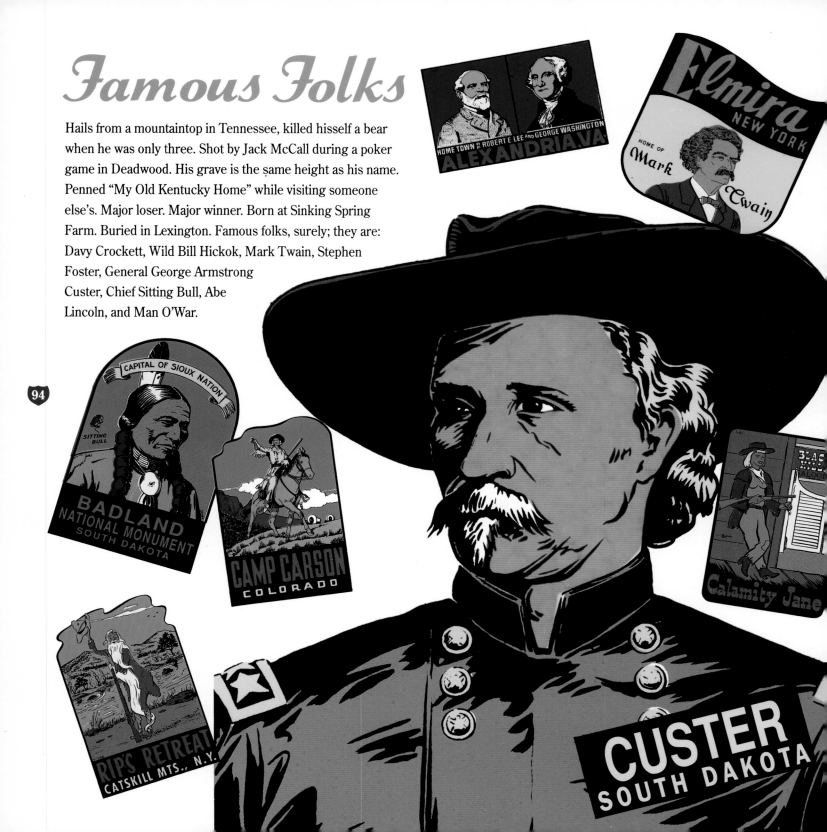

NOW YOU'VE SEEN A FLYING SAUCER

Thanks

We would like to thank the following for their help and support.

Abbeville Press: Walton Rawls, Hope Koturo, Renée Khatami

Rod Dyer Group, Inc.: Carolyn Baresic, Peter Cook, Dylan Dyer, Margaret Miyuki, Debbie Benedict, Allan Evenas, Cathy Herold, Joshua Mutchnick, Jo Sayama, Russell Oshita, Milly Quan, Terry Song, Qris Yamashita, Bill Murphy

Steve Sakai, Steve Breitborde, **Photography** • Brenda Lees, Dustin Lees, **Research**

Tommy Steele, Jim Heimann, Michael Doret, Ken Brown, **Collectors**

Special thanks to the Lindgren-Turner Co. and all decal manufacturers whose creations were the visual inspiration for our project.

Any omission of credit is inadvertent and will be corrected in future printings if notification is sent to the publisher.

96

LIKE MAN-ME WORRY?

YOUR BUMPER IS TOO CLOSE TO MINE!

AMERICA LOVE IT OR LEAVE IT

FT WALTON FLORIDA

DECALS for YOUR CAR

WALL DRUG STORE

WALL So. Dakota ON THE WALL OF THE SO. DAK. BADLAND